Local Church Membership

*'Righteousness,
Peace and Joy
in the Holy Spirit'*

by David W. Legg

Covenant Books UK

COVENANT BOOKS UK (CBUK)
10 Kelsey Close, Liss. GU33 7HR
Email: office@covenantbooksuk.org.uk
Website: https://covenantbooksuk.org.uk/
© David W. Legg 2023

First published by *Covenant Books UK* in 2023.

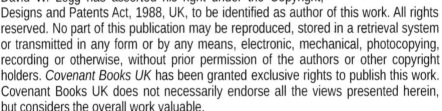

Note that occasionally, residual American spellings etc. have been corrected to English.

The cover illustration is based on a public domain photo of a fresco from the tomb of Vibia - Catacombs of Domitila, Rome, *An Agape 'Love' Feast* - © D.W. Legg 2023.

Created in *LibreOffice Community* 7.5.9.2 with open source software on *Fedora*™ *38 Linux*™.

Paperback ISBN: 9798870388588

To the members
and not-yet members
of Trinity Church Liphook

Many Christians struggle with the idea of church membership. This can mean that they do not join their local church as members. They so easily miss out on a huge range of spiritual and practical benefits.

This booklet explains why church membership is both biblical and beneficial, and how it results in *'righteousness, peace and joy in the Holy Spirit'* (Romans 14:17), blessings for believers, and glory for God.

It gives biblical, cultural and practical encouragement for Christians to join their local church as members. We must believe Jesus, who said, *"It is more blessed to give than to receive"* (Acts 20:35). Then we will grow as Christians and bring blessing to ourselves, our families, and to outsiders.

This booklet is suitable for members and non-members.

David Legg ministered in Devon (UK), and now lives and writes in Hampshire. He is married to Sue; they are members of Trinity Church Liphook, have three sons, a daughter-in-law and a grandson. His other books published by Covenant Books UK include:

• *Covenants for Evangelicals*

• *Humour in the Bible?*

• *The Right End of the Stick*

• *Reformed Evangelical Ministry Resources*

He has also compiled the following discussion Bible Study guides for small groups and individual use:

• *The Genesis Roller-coaster,*

• *The Exodus Experiment,*

• *1 and 2 Samuel,*

• *The Songs of Ascents and Eight Last Davidic Psalms (Psalms 120 to 145) and*

• *Ephesians.*

Contents

1 Introduction..7
  1.1 Historical background...7
  1.2 Doubts about membership.....................................9

2 'Think globally; act locally'....................................11
  2.1 The universal church..11
  2.2 The local church..12
  2.3 Joining the local church.......................................13

3 Membership and culture.......................................17
  3.1 Just another club?...17

4 Membership leads to blessing.............................19
  4.1 *More blessed to give* 19
  4.2 Christian maturity..21
  4.3 Family love..22

5 'Dos' and "Don'ts"..23
  5.1 Set a Christ-like example....................................23
  5.2 Be submissive...24
  5.3 Balanced 'Dos' and "Don'ts"...............................24

6 Why not join?..27
  6.1 Discipleship-Lite?...28
  6.2 How we view God's people..................................28
  6.3 The heart of the matter.......................................29
  6.4 The church itself?...30

7 Membership promises...31
  7.1 Promises for new members.................................31
  7.2 A promise for existing members..........................32

8 You might have asked 33
  8.1 Frequently Asked Questions................................33
  8.2 *'Righteousness, peace and joy'*.........................34

Appendix – Helpful list of 'Dos' and "don'ts"....................35

General Index...41

Scripture Index...43

1 Introduction

1.1 Historical background

In the recent past, Nonconformist[1] Evangelical churches have insisted on a very clear demarcation between local church 'members' and everyone else[2]. In practice, the list or 'roll' of members would include only those who were admitted to the Lord's supper, as can be seen in this moving account of a small revival in a 19th Century Devon (UK) village:

On 31st March, 1868, a church was formed, and fourteen [founding members] *united in Christian fellowship. …*

"We shall not soon forget the solemnity of the occasion, and the deeply impressive character of the whole scene. Although a week-day, the chapel was well filled, members of other village churches in the neighbourhood having come to manifest their interest and share the joy of the occasion. The communicants were seated on one side of the chapel, and the non-communicants on the other; and the eager look and tearful eyes testified that the latter had been led here by no mere curiosity. Some who had never before been present at a sacramental service [the Lord's supper], *confessed how deeply they were touched by that simple memorial of our Saviour's dying love.*

And after the service was over, several broken-hearted ones lingered behind and eagerly asked,

'What they must do to be saved?' …

---

1   Nonconformist simply means not Church of England.
2   This has not been the case within Anglicanism.

> *The effect of the revival, ... was in no wise transitory, for we learn that in 1870 the chapel was well filled at each service, and the interest and life of the church was fully sustained. The church roll* [of members] *had been steadily increasing, ...[3]*

Nowadays, in the 21st Century, the distinctions between members and non-members, communicants and non-communicants, tend to be more blurred. Such 'labelling' is seen as threatening and controlling, and is resisted in the names of individualism and freedom.

Many of those born since the 1960s have world-views that are conditioned by post-modernism, with its undermining of concepts such as authority, truth, revelation, importance, person-hood and reality[4]. Such world-views discourage Christians from thinking in terms of church membership, especially local church membership.

Thankfully, conservative Christians resist the tide of post-modernism by asking the question,

'What does the Bible say?'

So, is the notion of local church membership biblical? Would the apostle Paul approve? Did Jesus say anything on the subject?

Already, I am aware that I will be disturbing some who are reading this, who may take authoritative statements in scripture about church membership to be 'power-grabs', or attempts to control and exploit people.

And yet, what the Bible teaches, the things Jesus said, and what the apostles insisted on, are the only true guides to how a church should operate. So, in this booklet, the Bible will be taken as authoritative, and sometimes even prescriptive. It is, after all, better to be biblically correct (BC) than politically correct (PC).

---

3   *Historical Sketch of Lee Mill Independent Church and Congregation*, May, 1883; words of church secretary.
4   *Meltdown*, Making Sense of a Culture in Crisis, Marcus Honeysett, IVP, 2002.

1.2 Doubts about membership

Some things like water vapour in the atmosphere are real, but invisible; they only become visible later, in the case of water vapour, when it condenses and becomes rain.

Similarly, certain Christian teachings that are rehearsed every Sunday in creeds[5] and sermons are not that obvious in the Bible to the casual reader. So, for example, Christians believe in the Holy Trinity, but are not terribly clear where to find it taught in scripture. Few would consider these doctrines unbiblical, but there is an unhealthy lack of complete confidence in them.

Another such biblical teaching is that of membership in the local church. Indeed, there are two subjects therein: the local church, and church membership. But, whereas local *churches* mentioned in the Bible can easily be identified, for example,-

Romans 16:5 Greet also the church[6] [*that meets*, NIV] *in their house, ...*

the service where new members were welcomed-in is harder to spot; the interview by the elders, the church membership course, the promises made by new and existing members, are all only to be inferred[7] from scripture.

Then, there is the 'defeater belief'[8] that anything difficult, obscure or hard to understand in the Bible is so doubtful that it may not really be true; it can therefore be ignored or, at best, placed on the back-burner for the time being. Some would respond that it would be more godly simply to work a bit harder at understanding difficult teachings but, no, it is far easier and

---

5   Such as the doctrine of the Holy Trinity in the *Apostles' Creed*.

6   Greek: τὴν ἐκκλησίαν.

7   *Westminster Confession of Faith*, 1646/47, Para. 1(6): '*The whole counsel of God, concerning all things necessary for his own glory, man's salvation, faith, and life, is either expressly set down in scripture, or by good and necessary consequence may be deduced from scripture: unto which nothing at any time is to be added, whether by new revelations of the Spirit, or traditions of men.*'

8   An important idea, especially in evangelism, that some people's beliefs can render them incapable of taking an argument or doctrine seriously. This happens without them even entertaining the idea and completely, *defeats* any attempt to explain the it to them. Defeater beliefs have often been explained by Don Carson and the late Tim Keller in books and at conferences.

simpler to put them to the back of our minds. The underlying problem is, of course, not the difficulty or obscurity of the subject in scripture, but human nature, our natural laziness. Indeed, it is a sin of omission, a failure to prioritise God's kingdom as Jesus said we should:

Matthew 6:33 But seek first the kingdom of God and his right-eousness, and all these things will be added to you.

This is a key verse in Christian discipleship[9], and exposes our heart attitudes and motivation. For whom are we living, brothers and sisters, ourselves or Jesus?

So, let us proceed by looking first at membership of the universal church. Then, let us narrow it down to the local church, and find specific biblical teaching about becoming a church member, how membership interacts with our culture, what it looks like in practice, its benefits and its motivations, all the while basing our exploration on Bible texts that are neither obscure, unimportant, nor hard to find.

---

9   The word 'disciple' (Greek: μαθητής) (mathētēs) conveys mainly a NT idea of a follower, learner, and one who seeks to be like his or her master. Ultimately it is Christians who are Jesus' disciples.

2 'Think globally; act locally'

2.1 The universal church

Every true Christian is already a *member* of the universal church, as we discover from the apostle Paul:

Ephesians 3:6 ... the Gentiles are fellow heirs [with the Jews], *members of the same body, and partakers of the promise in Christ Jesus through the gospel.*

Paul likens the universal church to a *body*, specifically *Christ's body*. In the same way that a human *body* has *members* such as hands and feet, so *Christ's* universal church has *members*–Christians. These are scattered throughout time and have no particular geographical location. They gradually find their way to heaven and the new earth where their full number will eventually be reached, and remain for ever.

The universal church is a valid and important concept, but tangible discipleship[9] and fellowship only take place here on earth in a local church. It is impossible to serve the universal church, worship with it[10], be an elder or deacon in it, administer the sacraments in it or be disciplined by it. To say, "I am a member of the universal church", has almost no practical meaning in terms of how we should 'do' and 'be' church from day to day. It is only when we "think globally, but act locally" (as environmentalists sometimes say) that we begin to bless each other and impact the local community, here on earth, for Christ.

---

10   Despite our *mystic, sweet communion—The church's one foundation (Samuel Stone),* and Hebrews 12:22.

2.2 The local church

As noted previously, there are numerous examples of local churches in the New Testament (NT) (Romans 16:5; 1 Corinthians 16:19; Philemon 2). But does the NT demonstrate or teach the idea of local church membership, and of people joining and leaving? The answer is 'yes', and that the NT explicitly supports the idea of joining a local church. We will trace the ideas of 'church' and membership from what Jesus said whilst teaching here on earth, through into the events recorded in Acts, after Jesus had returned to heaven, but was still working on earth through his apostles.

First, we must notice that sometimes what Jesus said related to the universal church; for example:

Matthew 16:18 ... I will build my church[11], and the gates of hell shall not prevail against it.

This refers in the first place to the universal church, but even this promise is fulfilled in practice here on earth through local churches being established and built.[12]

On another occasion, secondly, Jesus spoke about something that only makes sense in the context of a local church, where someone has become in need of some (negative) church discipline[13]:

Matthew 18:16 If he [the unrepentant sinner] *refuses to listen to them* [one or two others] *tell it to the church[14]. And if he refuses to listen even to the church[15] let him be to you as a Gentile and a tax collector.*

In other words, suspend his rights as a church member and treat him as a non-Christian.[16] Terms such as 'excommunicate'

---

11   Greek: ἐκκλησίαν.
12   The word '*church*' (Greek: ἐκκλησία) in the Bible is never a building, but always people.
13   The majority of church discipline is 'positive' and happens through fellowship and the teaching of God's word, but where this fails, negative measures are to be taken.
14   Greek: τῇ ἐκκλησίᾳ
15   Greek: τῆς ἐκκλησίας
16   The Jewishness of Jesus' social context meant that referring to Non-Christians as *Gentiles* made sense to his immediate hearers, as did the term *tax collector*!

or even 'church discipline' [13] had not been invented at this stage of church history, but Jesus' instruction means the same. We can readily recognise the ideas of being 'in' the church, then 'out' of it. This would be impossible at the level of the universal church, and can only be done locally (see also 1 Corinthians 5:12-13). We will now see how these ideas of becoming 'in' or 'out' of a local church are developed further, in the book of Acts.

2.3 Joining the local church

The first NT local church was established in Jerusalem, and Dr Luke[17] speaks of people being '*added*' to it (Acts 2:41,47; 5:14[18]). In chapter 5, after the shocking sin and summary execution of *Ananias and Sapphira*, a definite delineation appears between those who were 'in' the church, and those who were 'out':

Acts 5:12b ... they were all together in Solomon's Portico. [13a]
None of the rest dared join [fn 19] *them, but the people held them in high esteem.*

The local church was meeting in part of the temple (*Solomon's Portico*). Not only were the Christians terrified (Acts 5:11), so was everyone else (v12). So, there was a distinction enforced by a combination of fear and *high esteem*, between Christians and non-Christians,

members and outsiders, such that unbelievers did not *dare* to '*join*' the local church. Perhaps for the first time, our modern usage of the word '*join*' to describe becoming a church member is the same as the biblical usage.

Moving on from negative examples, in Acts 9, *Saul* has recently

---

17   Luke wrote Acts.
18   Greek: προστίθημι
19   Greek: κολλᾶσθαι

been converted in a dynamic display of Jesus' power (and is *baptised* by a rather scared and unwilling disciple[9], *Ananias*). By the regenerating work of God the Holy Spirit, *Saul* has now joined the universal church of Christ.

For a while, *Saul* tries to serve God on his own; he preaches and argues mainly with other Jews that *Jesus is the Son of God* (Acts 9:20-22).

Having gained some followers, made many enemies, and nearly been killed, he is smuggled out of *Damascus* and goes to *Jerusalem*. Why there? Because *Jerusalem* is where the *church* is. Presumably (and we can deduce these points from how things turn out), he wanted to:

a) Make himself available to serve the local *church* in *Jerusalem* as he had in *Damascus*;

b) enjoy the benefits of belonging to the local *church* (including some protection, perhaps?); and

c) subject himself to the authority of the local *church*.

And so, we read:

Acts 9:26a And when he had come to Jerusalem, he attempted to join [fn 20] *the disciples.*

So let us be clear about this, previously he had become a member of the universal *church* but not a member of the local *church* in *Jerusalem*. But, Dr Luke[17] tells us that *Saul* wanted to *join* them. How such joining would have been practised, formally and administratively, we are not told. And presumably it would have been determined culturally in some way that was natural to the church of the day. But the major reason that we are not told is because his 'application for church membership', as we might term it, was rejected! Why?

Acts 9:26b ... they were all afraid of him,

*   for they did not believe that he was a disciple.*[9]

So, *Saul's* first experience of the local *church* was of its

---

20   Greek: κολλᾶσθαι

authority (See c) above)! Sadly, in this case, it was a misuse of authority, or at least a mismanagement of *Saul's* request to *join* the local *church*.

Barnabas comes to the rescue and makes a case for *Saul* having a credible profession of faith. He goes over the heads of the local *church* authorities. *Saul* is accepted and put to work straight away as an evangelist in *Jerusalem* (Acts 9:27).

Although much of this is culturally alien to us, it nevertheless demonstrates an attempt to *join* a geographically located, local *church*. The fact that Saul's first attempt failed only serves to emphasise that local church membership is real. Barnabas' assistance and the apostles' intervention show that it matters.

Negatively, Matthew 18:16 (see page 12) teaches us that local church membership can be cancelled or, at least, suspended. But, the verses that we have visited in Acts show us that membership of the universal *church* should be expressed by *joining* a local *church*.

As Teddy Roosevelt[21] famously said,

"Do what you can, with what you have, where you are."

Likewise, Saul was not content simply to say to himself, 'I am a member of the universal church.' He wanted to join a local church so that he could make himself available to serve real people, in a real place. He wanted real fellowship in a local church with all the benefits and demands. He had become, after all, not just a consumer, but a disciple[9] (Matthew 28:19).

We will look at membership in the context of our consumer-oriented culture in the next chapter ...

---

21   President of the United States of America from 1901 to 1909.

3 Membership and culture

Given that the notion of joining a local church is taught in scripture, and is exemplified by the newly converted Saul[22], as we saw in the previous chapter, we must decide what that looks like, for us, in the 21st Century.

Saul trying to join a local church in Acts 9 did not necessarily involve being added to a formal list of members. Having lists of members is a modern, middle class, western, thing to do; it is part of our culture[23]. The question for us today is therefore, "How do we take Acts 9:26a and do it ourselves in the 21st century, western, church?" [23]

3.1 Just another club?

Normally, if we want to enjoy the benefits of a social organisation like a golf club or the *Women's Institute*[24] (WI), we have to join it. Indeed, the front page of the WI website immediately presents a woman with a button to click-on entitled '*Become a Member or Supporter*'. She must gain approval from the existing members, have her name added to the list of members, join in with the normal life of the organisation, and keep its rules. It would be odd if church membership were any less organised.

It is therefore very natural and culturally appropriate for 21st century churches to have formal membership lists. This is how

---

22   Before he became known as the apostle Paul in Acts 13:9.
23   I'm assuming that you are reading this somewhere in the western world; if not please accept my apologies and keep following the argument.
24   https://www.thewi.org.uk/

the biblical model of joining a local church is contextualised[25] in a way that is inoffensive to modern, western, people. Having a list makes membership sufficiently formal for it to be taken seriously by everyone. At the same time, nothing culturally alien or old fashioned is imposed unnecessarily on the modern, western,[23] Christian.

If someone seems commitment-shy and therefore unwilling to join a local church, but does seem to have a credible profession of faith in Christ, I would want to ask questions like-

"What clubs are you a member of?"

"What organisations do you belong to?"

"Do you have a bank or building society membership?"

"What social media organisations do you have an account for?"

"How is joining a local congregation of God's people less attractive, less beneficial, less important, less valuable, less biblical etc?"

But, the church is not just another club, and it is never less than a club:

Ephesians 5:25 ... Christ loved the church and gave himself up for her, ...

An 'agape' (love) feast
from the Roman Catacombs (public domain)

---

25   i.e. Brought from being a biblical principle, to being done appropriately in a culture, without sacrificing any of the essence, but by making it doable by people who live in the culture.

4 Membership leads to blessing

When tomato plants look pale, they need more nitrogen; when they fail to fruit, they need more potassium; when the leaves go yellow, they need more magnesium. What causes the spiritual and emotional growth of Christians to be stunted?

My own observations would suggest two very common maladies:

a) a failure to make good use of the available means of God's grace, including prayer, reading scripture, the sacraments, fellowship, etc., and

b) a failure to commit to joining a local church.

Why might the latter impair spiritual growth?

4.1 *More blessed to give ...*

When Christians join a church they immediately start to receive more, and better, family-type blessings than mere attenders receive. They are consistently prayed for; the get encouraging accountability, warmer fellowship, lasting friendship, long-term support, practical help, proper care, a healthy sense of family responsibility, numerous opportunities, that elusive sense of belonging, fresh kingdom-oriented desires, etc. The list goes on and on.

Furthermore, in the same way that the Lord Jesus said,

'It is more blessed to give than to receive' (Acts 20:35),

so the new church member also gains many opportunities to *give*, and hence *receive* even more blessing.

By joining a church, the Christian is saying,

"Here I am, give me a job; allow me to share in the work."

In the light of Acts 20:35, this could almost be seen as selfish! Indeed John Piper provocatively calls this sort of thing 'Christian hedonism'.[26] Why? Because the more we give, the more we are blessed. The more we exercise faith, the more we grow. The more we use our gifts, the more joy we have.

When we just turn up to church now and then, in consumer mode, certainly we receive a little, hit-and-miss, blessing from attending, mixing with Christians, benefiting from the means of grace. But when we become church members we are able to start giving in new, fresh and encouraging ways. And, as Jesus said, then the blessing really starts to flow-to others, yes, but to ourselves as well. And the more we give, the more we get. Not only does our future heavenly reward increase, but we get the pleasure of seeing those around us benefit and grow, we know more of the Holy Spirit's presence and help, we experience joy that non-members can only dream about.

I would not want to be accused of advocating a health, wealth and prosperity gospel, but church members who give financially frequently find that God blesses them even more, often financially. This would seem to be very much in line with Jesus' words:

Luke 16:10 "Whoever can be trusted with very little can also be trusted with much, and whoever is dishonest with very little will also be dishonest with much. [11] So if you have not been trust-worthy in handling worldly wealth, who will trust you with true riches? [12] And if you have not been trustworthy with someone

---

26   *Desiring God:* Meditations of a Christian Hedonist, John Piper, 2003, *Multnomah Books*

else's property, who will give you property of your own?[27]

It would seem that, from time to time, Jesus gives his people a taste of this principle even in the here and now.

4.2 Christian maturity

Furthermore, when you are a church member, you feel more of an obligation to serve, give, love, help and even just to turn up reliably to meetings. This sense of responsibility, when combined with faith, guarantees that the member engages more with church life, benefits more, receives more, grows as a Christian, grows as a person, and matures spiritually.

I have coined the term 'kollaophobia'[28]–the fear of joining–in order to name this problem, and bring it out into the light for honest examination here and in later chapters. People who do not overcome their kollaophobia, never quite seem to grow up (see Ephesians 4:13 on maturity). They feel they can only have by keeping, but Jesus makes it clear that the way to get is by giving (Acts 20:35).

A worked example of this is found in the a closely related area of church life, where Paul is telling Timothy how to go about appointing deacons. He writes:

1 Timothy 3:8 Deacons likewise must be [list of qualifications] ... [13] *For those who serve well as deacons gain a good stand-ing for themselves and also great confidence* [*assurance* NIV] *in the faith that is in Christ Jesus.* ESV

He is saying that deacons *gain* by giving, grow by *serving*[29]. They give time, effort, service, care, etc., but they *gain a good standing* and *great confidence* [*assurance* NIV]. So, there are even tangible, felt, blessings from giving, serving and caring. This *great confidence* is presumably a sense of *assurance* of

---

27   Not forgetting Jesus' warning – Luke 16:13 *"No one can serve two masters. Either you will hate the one and love the other, or you will be devoted to the one and despise the other. You cannot serve both God and money"* (ESV). The NIV makes it clear that this is the god Mammon by capitalising the word *'Money'*.

28   From the Greek verbs κολλάω (kollaō) 'join' + φοβέω (phobeō) 'fear'.

29   Indeed, the Greek word for 'deacon', διάκονος, means 'servant'.

sins forgiven and perhaps a boldness in sharing the gospel. These are the kinds of things that many Christians long for during their quiet times, but then allow their kollaophobia[28] to prevent them taking the first step of asking if they can join their local church properly, as members.

4.3 Family love

As individuals, becoming mature believers is a great protection against falling into major sin. But it is when we see ourselves not just as individuals but as part of a family that the local church functions best, most biblically, most lovingly. This means that when church members get into some sort of trouble, sin, and then disappear from church, their absence is noticed. Their absence is felt and they are automatically looked-for, cared-about, visited and, hopefully, loved back into fellowship, regardless of how far they have strayed. It is important to see the word 'love' in the Bible an action word, not just a gooey feeling. Feelings are great, godly motivations are important, but love means doing something, as demonstrated by *God*:

John 3:16 This is how God loved the world: He gave his only Son … ESV MARGIN.

The blessing of having a loving church family that will not let you go is something that non-members do not have:

Jude 23 save others by snatching them out of the fire; …

It is easily assumed that when non-members disappear they have simply gone to another church. Furthermore, the church leadership cannot easily insist on visiting or helping non-members. If the blessing of (negative) church discipline[13] is needed, it is likely that only members will benefit. This is not the main blessing of being a church member, but it is a significant one. Being a church member is being a family member. Being a church member is a bit like being legally married instead of just 'living together'.

5 'Dos' and "Don'ts"

Whilst we should never slip into a Pharisaical way of living in which we somehow relate to God and each other through a set of rules, the commands in scripture are there to help us live in a way that brings glory to God and expresses love to the local church family.

5.1 Set a Christ-like example

John 13:15 For I [Jesus] *have given you an example, that you also should do just as I have done to you.*

In the same way that Jesus has set us an *example* to follow[30], so there are many commands to set or follow a good *example* in the NT, e.g.:

Philippians 3:17 Join together in following my example, brothers and sisters, and just as you have us as a model, keep your eyes on those who live as we do.

Such verses remind us that not only should we follow good *examples*, but also, as church members, we must set a good *example* for others to follow. We are always being watched by other members, non-members, our children and grandchildren, non-Christians, complete outsiders, neighbours, colleagues, friends, by everyone really. Often the perceived credibility of the gospel depends on the example set by church members.

---

30   Specifically, on that occasion, by washing his disciples' feet. But, more generally, this teaches all disciples to be humble enough to serve each other. See the 'each other' verses in the 'Dos' and "Don'ts" appendix.

5.2 Be submissive

A specific responsibility appears at the end of Hebrews:

Heb 13:17a Be guided[31] by your leaders and submit to them, because they keep watch over you as those who will have to give account. DWL

Then the writer[32] gives the motivation for such submission:

Hebrews 13:17b Do this so that their work will be a joy, not a burden, for that would be of no benefit to you. NIV

So we should be guided by our church leaders e.g. to apply for church membership, to co-operate with whatever promises they ask us to make when joining, to turn up to events they organise, to serve in various ways.

5.3 Balanced 'Dos' and "Don'ts"

How Christians should relate to each other in the local church and more widely is dealt with extensively in the NT using the phrase 'each other'[33] or 'one another'.[33] There are prohibitions and warnings, but mainly encouragements and commands.

These texts are overwhelmingly positive, which happens to fit in well with what people naturally prefer. But most of them are also divine commands, and so, should be taken most seriously. Each text bears careful reflection by both new and existing church members. They mostly speak for themselves, but there are quite a lot of them so they have been put in an appendix starting on page 35 for you to use in slow-time, perhaps as the basis for a week's worth of quiet times?

They are not simply a long list telling us to serve (John 13:14), love (John 13:34-35) and encourage (Romans 1:12) etc. The key, really, is to learn to think in terms of *'each other'*. If we can

---

31 The ESV has *'Obey your leaders'* (which is a little too direct to be sustainable by the original word), the NIV has *'have confidence'*, which is perhaps a little too indirect. The Greek word, Πείθεσθε, can mean *'Be persuaded by'*. Whilst this implies obedience, it does not actually mean 'obey'. The writer's usage in Hebrews 2:13, 6:9 and also 13:18 are instructive. Also, note that the verse says *'submit'*.

32 See https://davidlegg.org.uk/our_brother_timothy.html for a possible identity of the writer.

33 Greek: ἀλλήλους

do that we will be fruitful and godly church members.

The list of "don'ts" is not just a list of forbidden behaviours, but a helpful set of reminders or warnings that will guard us from those occasions when we forget to think in terms of *'each other'*.

There are fewer "don'ts" than 'dos', but the "don'ts" are no less important. We should not be put off by society's aversion to negatives; both negatives and positives are needed for a wise balance.

Based on a fresco from the tomb of Vibia - Catacombs of Domitila – Rome
An Agape 'Love' Feast - © D.W. Legg 2023

6 Why not join?

Having discussed how local church membership is both biblically correct and culturally appropriate, we now turn to the subject of attitudes and difficulties that may prevent Christians from joining their local church.

Fear is a destructive emotion in many contexts, and the fear of joining a local church is a widespread phenomenon. Such kollaophobia[34] may come from genuine fears of being controlled in wrong or unbiblical ways, including past experiences of 'heavy shepherding[35]' or abuse. It may also stem from our own attitudes, including pride, a lack of submissiveness, or from a desire always to be the one in control.

So, what are the main things that might prevent us from throwing in our lot with God's people locally nowadays?

---

34   See page 21 for a definition of this term. From the Greek verbs κολλάω (kollaō) 'join' + φοβέω (phobeō) 'fear'.

35   It is clear from 1 Peter 5:1-5 that church leaders are to 'shepherd' the flock. However, this is for the good of the flock, not harm, and not for their own ends. Even worse than such bad shepherding is the cultish practice of 'heavy shepherding', which controls people's finances, time, and decisions in a way that it is abusive, often illegal and psychologically manipulative to the serious detriment of victims.

6.1 Discipleship-Lite?

When Jesus gave us, his church, the great commission in Matthew 28:19, he did not simply say, "evangelise", he said *"make disciples"*.[36] This is more than getting people to believe; it is more than baptising them. The next verse adds:

Matthew 28:20 ... 'teaching them to observe all that I have commanded' ...

So, if you are a true disciple[9], you will want to *observe all* the *teaching* that Jesus gave through his apostles, including all the passages in previous chapters that relate to the subject of local church membership.

If you don't, could it be that you are not yet a genuine disciple?[9]

A selection of drinks; some are 'lite' ...

6.2 How we view God's people

When Ruth the Moabitess wanted the LORD to be her *God*, she understood that this also meant making God's *people* her *people*. She said to Naomi:

Ruth 1:16 "Your people will be my people
*   and your God my God".*

This is the basic piece of evidence from the book of Ruth that showed that she was now trusting the LORD for herself. She was throwing her lot in with *God's people*. Our attitude to God's

---

36   Greek: μαθητεύσατε, verb meaning 'disciple' or even 'discipline'!

people is a barometer of our attitude to God himself. As Jesus said:

1 John 4:12 No one has ever seen God;
> [but] *if we love one another,*
>> *God abides in us*
>> *and his love is perfected* [i.e. made visible] *in us.*

There is therefore a direct connection between our commitment to Jesus Christ (who is God) and our commitment to each other. Any thoughts such as, 'It's not Christ who is the problem; it is the Christians', point the finger straight back at ourselves and our heart-attitudes.

In those days, there was only one local church–the people of Israel[37], so Ruth committed; she joined.

6.3 The heart of the matter

That church membership is a matter of the heart can be seen from the emotional words that *Ruth* uses when Naomi tries to send her away from *God* and his *people*:

Ruth 1:16 But Ruth said,

> *"Do not urge me to leave you*
>> *or to return from following you* [Naomi]*.*

> *For where you go I will go,*
>> *and where you lodge I will lodge.*

> *Your people shall be my people,*
>> *and your God my God."*

And as if that were somehow not enough to convince Naomi, she makes a *death*-vow(!) in the name of *the LORD*:

[17] *"Where you die I will die,*
> *and there will I be buried.*
May the LORD do so to me and more also
> *if anything but death parts me from you."*

---

37   This is made clear by the 76 references to the church (ἐκκλησία, ekklēsia) in the Greek OT (LXX), and also in Stephen's speech in Acts 7 where he talks about Moses being *'in the church* (ἐκκλησίᾳ) *in the wilderness"*

Notice how Ruth's heart is directed not only towards *God*, but towards Naomi herself and towards Naomi's *people*, God's *people*. Ruth's vow perhaps shows us that it is biblical for new church members to make promises to the local congregation.

Ruth had to decide whether she was going back to Moab and the god Chemosh with her sister-in-law. She showed that her faith was real by committing herself instead to *the LORD'S people*.

As noted previously, there was only one local church–the people of Israel[37], so she committed; she joined. Despite the huge emotional wrench of leaving her own family, religion and culture, she overcame any kollaophobia[34] and forced[38] her way into the kingdom of God, dismissing Naomi's attempts at counter-evangelism.

Local church leaders need to challenge hangers-on to be a little introspective, to be biblical about their view of the local church, and to repent of whatever might keep them from joining.

6.4 The church itself?

Some churches exclude genuine Christians from membership even though they are not under any kind of negative church discipline[13]. There is probably nothing you can do about this.

There may also be areas of church life or polity that present potential members with obstacles to joining. In these cases, the leadership may need to review church practice. Or it may be sufficient for them simply to assure potential members that they don't have to agree with absolutely everything, just to submit peaceably to the way the church is run (see Romans 15:7).

It is said, "If you find the perfect church, don't join it because you'll spoil it!" Or, to put it another way: You will never find a perfect church, but join anyway, as a humble sinner.

---

38   Luke 16:16.

7 Membership promises

The following are typical questions used for bringing a Christian into local church membership. However, they vary from church to church, denomination to denomination.

7.1 Promises for new members

The first question asks you to affirm belief in the basics of the historic and biblical Christian faith, thereby aligning yourself with believers throughout twenty centuries.

Q. 1. *Do you worship one God in three persons, the Father, Son and Holy Spirit, and do you believe that God the Son is fully both God and [hu]man?*

The second question relates to the substitutionary atonement made by Jesus on the cross.

Q. 2. *Are you relying on Christ's death on the cross in your place to pay the penalty for your sins?*

The third question asks you to confess a personal and on-going faith in Jesus. It also rejects any self-reliance.

Q. 3. *Are you trusting in Christ alone for your salvation, and not in anything you yourself can do?*

The fourth question narrows down your commitment to a specific local church (for the time-being), but this is still something to be done by trusting God, not merely an administrative change.

Q. 4. *Will you serve Christ as part of this local church, realising that it may be costly, and can only be done by relying daily on God's strength?*

An essential part of church unity and effectiveness for God's kingdom is a willingness to be guided by those in authority in the local church, to submit to their plans and requests etc.

Q. 5. *Do you recognise the authority of the church leadership [or elders]?*

Church membership involves loving each other and outsiders in a 'hands-on' and prayerful way.

Q. 6. *Will you support this congregation by prayer, by giving as you are able, and by caring practically for individuals?*

Church membership is not only about relating well to the leadership, but to all church members, and also to outsiders.

Q. 7. *Do you commit yourself to foster healthy relationships in this congregation, recognising that this includes*
a) the stifling of gossip, and
b) the expression of needful criticism in a loving and humble manner?

7.2 A promise for existing members

The following question is for the existing members of the church who are present. Usually, the leader presiding over the occasion will ask them to stand up and promise to all the new members:

Q. 8. *Will you accept and welcome these new members, supporting them lovingly, practically and prayerfully?*

Answer: We will, [and may Almighty God receive the thanks and glory.]

8 You might have asked …

8.1 Frequently Asked Questions

FAQ 1 *Does joining a local church mean that I cannot visit any other church?*
Absolutely not; visiting other churches can enlarge our vision, strengthen fellowship and provide variety. However, part of your commitment to one local church includes reasonably regular attendance at its meetings, willingness to be on rôtas etc.

FAQ 2 *Is church membership 'till death us do part'?*
No; it is normal for Christians to move from one church to another, sometimes even changing denomination. But this should always be done prayerfully, and considering what is best for God's kingdom, our families and each other. Sometimes a church will send a letter of commendation to the new church.

FAQ 3 *I have previously been in a church where the leadership did what is commonly known as 'heavy shepherding'[35]. How can I be sure that this church will not be in any way abusive or controlling?*
You can't. But the behaviour referred to is ungodly, sinful, and such leaders need to be rebuked by someone. If they are not repentant, you should seek further recourse, from other church members, elders or church leaders.

FAQ 4 *Can I be a member of more than one local church?*
No. See the typical questions in the 7 'Membership promises'.

FAQ 5 *What if I don't entirely agree with the church's basis of faith, practice or constitution (trust deed or other founding documents)?*
You will need to be interviewed by the local church leadership to

discuss these matters. It will normally be possible to accommodate any true believer. You may find that you need to be content to co-operate whilst not always agreeing. Remaining a non-member as a form of protest may not be godly. Helpful verses to consider include:

1 Corinthians 1:17 For Christ did not send me to baptise, but to preach the gospel, ... NIV

Romans 14:17 For the kingdom of God is not a matter of eating and drinking but of righteousness and peace and joy in the Holy Spirit.

8.2 'Righteousness, peace and joy'

Notice that last verse, Romans 14:17: *'Righteousness, ... peace and joy'* are what church membership is all about, because they are what God's *kingdom* is all about-

1. Church membership encourages and ensures that we make the best possible use of the various means of grace to grow us all to maturity (page 21). 'Maturity' is just another way of saying practical **righteousness** (see Hebrews 5:13).

2. As Proverbs 12:20 tells us, *'those who plan* **peace** *have* **joy**'. **Peace** in each local church is of great importance and usually depends on how we relate to *'one another'*. But, as we peaceably use our gifts to serve others in faith so we receive *joy in the Holy Spirit* as one of his *fruit*(s) (Galatians 5:22).

3. Finally, that sense of *assurance* (NIV) or *confidence* (ESV) (1 Timothy 3:8-13) discussed on page 21 is certainly not limited (Hebrews 10:22; 11:1) to deacons, and is the normal experience of church members.

From The Three Graces by Rafaelo 1483–1520 - Re-purposed

Appendix – Helpful list of 'Dos' and "don'ts"

'DOS', OR COMMANDS	
Luke 24:14	*… they were talking with each other about all these things that had happened.* – the cross and resurrection. – We too should talk about spiritually profitable things.
Luke 24:32	*They said to each other "Did not our hearts burn within us while he talked to us on the road, while he opened to us the scriptures?"* – We should check that our hearts still warm to the scriptures and, if not, repent, asking that Jesus would once again speak to us.
John 13:14	*"If I then, your Lord and Teacher, have washed your feet you also ought to wash one another's feet."* – Humble service of each other.
John 13:34-35	*"A new commandment I give to you that you love one another: just as I have loved you, you also are to love one another. [35] By this all people will know that you are my disciples [fn 9], if you have love for one another."*
Romans 1:12	*… be mutually encouraged by each other's faith, both yours and mine.*
Romans 12:5	*… we, though many are one body in Christ, and individually members one of another.* – Something always to remember. – Not limited to the local church.
Romans 12:10	*Love one another with brotherly affection. Outdo one another in showing honour.*
Romans 12:16	*Live in harmony with one another. Do not be haughty, but associate with the lowly. Never be wise in your own*

	'DOS', OR COMMANDS
	sight.
Romans 13:8	*Owe no one anything, except to love each other, for the one who loves another has fulfilled the law.*
Romans 14:13	*Therefore let us not pass judgement on one another any longer, but rather decide never to put a stumbling block or hindrance in the way of a brother.*
Romans 14:19	*Let us therefore make every effort to do what leads to peace and to mutual edification.* NIV
Romans 15:5	*May the God who gives endurance and encouragement give you the same attitude of mind toward each other that Christ Jesus had, …* NIV
Romans 15:7	*Therefore welcome one another as Christ has welcomed you, for the glory of God.*
Romans 15:14	*I myself am satisfied about you, my brothers that you yourselves are full of goodness, filled with all knowledge and able to instruct one another.* – This is at least something to aspire to.
Romans 16:16	*Greet one another with a holy kiss. All the churches of Christ greet you.* – Our mutual greetings should be warm and genuine.
1 Corinthians 7:5	*Do not deprive one another, except perhaps by agreement for a limited time, that you may devote yourselves to prayer; but then come together again so that Satan may not tempt you because of your lack of self-control.* – Particularly applies to marriage.
1 Corinthians 12:25	*… that there may be no division in the body, but that the members may have the same care for one another.*
Galatians 5:13	*For you were called to freedom, brothers. Only do not use your freedom as an opportunity for the flesh, but through love serve one another.*
Galatians 6:2	*Bear one another's burdens, and so fulfil the law of Christ.*
Ephesians 4:2	[Live in] *all humility and gentleness, with patience bearing with one another in love,*
Ephesians 4:25	*Therefore, having put away falsehood, let each one of*

	'DOS', OR COMMANDS
	you speak the truth with his neighbour, for we are members one of another.
Ephesians 4:32	*Be kind to one another, tender-hearted forgiving one another, as God in Christ forgave you.*
Ephesians 5:21	*… submitting to one another out of reverence for Christ.* - Applies to various relationships. See Ephesians 5:21-6:9 for the context.
Philippians 2:3	*Do nothing from selfish ambition or conceit, but in humility count others more significant than yourselves.*
Colossians 3:9	*Do not lie to one another, seeing that you have put off the old self with its practices …*
Colossians 3:13	*… bearing with one another and if one has a complaint against another forgiving each other; as the Lord has forgiven you, so you also must forgive.*
1 Thessalonians 3:12	*… may the Lord make you increase and abound in love for one another and for all, as we do for you, …*
1 Thessalonians 4:9	*Now concerning brotherly love you have no need for anyone to write to you, for you yourselves have been taught by God to love one another, …*
1 Thessalonians 4:18; 5:11	*Therefore encourage one another with these words.* [Again, check the immediate context.] [11] *… encourage one another and build one another up, just as you are doing.*
2 Thessalonians 1:3	*We ought always to give thanks to God for you, brothers as is right, because your faith is growing abundantly, and the love of every one of you for one another is increasing.* – Thanksgiving for each other is important.
Hebrews 10:24-25	*And let us consider how to stir up one another to love and good works,* [25] *not neglecting to meet together, as is the habit of some, but encouraging one another, and all the more as you see the Day drawing near.*
James 5:16	*Therefore confess your sins to each other and pray for each other so that you may be healed. The prayer of a righteous person is powerful and effective.* NIV
1 Peter 1:22	*Having purified your souls by your obedience to the*

'DOS', OR COMMANDS	
	truth for a sincere brotherly love, love one another earnestly from a pure heart, …
1 Peter 4:9	*Show hospitality to one another without grumbling.*
1 Peter 5:5	*… Clothe yourselves, all of you, with humility toward one another, for "God opposes the proud but gives grace to the humble."*
1 John 1:7	*But if we walk in the light as he is in the light, we have fellowship with one another, and the blood of Jesus his Son cleanses us from all sin.*
1 John 3:11	*For this is the message that you have heard from the beginning that we should love one another.*
1 John 3:23	*And this is his commandment that we believe in the name of his Son Jesus Christ and love one another just as he has commanded us.*
1 John 4:7	*Dear friends, let us love one another, for love comes from God. Everyone who loves has been born of God and knows God. NIV*
1 John 4:11	*… if this is how God loved us, we also ought to love one another. DWL*
1 John 4:12	*No one has ever seen God; if we love one another, God abides in us and his love is perfected* [i.e. made visible] *in us.*
2 John 5	*And now I ask you, dear lady* [presumably, a church]— *not as though I were writing you a new commandment, but the one we have had from the beginning—that we love one another.*

"DON'TS" AND WARNINGS	
Matthew 24:10	*"And then many will fall away and betray one another and hate one another."* - When persecution comes.
Mark 9:34	*But they kept silent, for on the way they had argued with one another about who was the greatest.*
Mark 9:50	*"Salt is good but if the salt has lost its saltiness, how will you make it salty again? Have salt in yourselves, and be at peace with one another."*
John 5:43	*How can you believe, when you receive glory from one another and do not seek the glory that comes from the only God?*
John 6:43	*'Stop grumbling among yourselves,'* *Jesus answered.* NIV
Acts 7:26	*The next day Moses came upon two Israelites who were fighting. He tried to reconcile them by saying, "Men, you are brothers; why do you want to hurt each other?"* NIV
Acts 15:39	*And there arose a sharp disagreement, so that they separated from each other. Barnabas took Mark with him and sailed away to Cyprus, …*
Acts 28:4	*When the native people saw the creature hanging from [Paul's] hand, they said to one another "No doubt this man is a murderer. Though he has escaped from the sea Justice has not allowed him to live."* – We must avoid such hasty judgements.
Romans 1:27	*… men likewise gave up natural relations with women and were consumed with passion for one another men committing shameless acts with men and receiving in themselves the due penalty for their error.* – the avoidance of sexual immorality like the pagans
1 Corinthians 11:33	*So then, my brothers, when you come together to eat, wait for one another …* – The Lord's supper must be orderly, loving and circumspect.
Galatians 5:15	*But if you bite and devour one another, watch out that you are not consumed by one another.*
Galatians 5:26	*Let us not become conceited, provoking one another,*

"DON'TS" AND WARNINGS	
	envying one another.
1 Thessalonians 5:15	*See that no one repays anyone evil for evil, but always seek to do good to one another and to everyone.*
Titus 3:3	*For we ourselves were once foolish, disobedient, led astray, slaves to various passions and pleasures, passing our days in malice and envy, hated by others and hating one another.* *– Humbly remember how we were.*
James 4:11	*Do not speak evil against one another, brothers. The one who speaks against a brother or judges his brother, speaks evil against the law and judges the law. But if you judge the law, you are not a doer of the law but a judge.*
James 5:9	*Do not grumble against one another, brothers, so that you may not be judged; behold, the Judge is standing at the door.*

Please see the table of **Contents** on page 5.

Please check the **General Index** (page 41) for subjects without obvious headings in the table of contents.

The **Scripture Index** (page 43) allows you to work backwards from Bible texts to their use in this booklet.

General Index

Abuse...................................27
Accountability.....................19
Ambition.............................37
America.................................2
Anglicanism..........................7
Apostle.................8, 12, 15, 28
Apostles' Creed.....................9
Applying for church
    membership........14, 22, 24
Arguing...............................39
Assurance.......................21, 34
Attitude.........10, 27, 28, 29, 36
Authority..............8, 14, 15, 32
Bank or building society.......18
Baptism...........................14, 28
Barnabas........................15, 39
Bearing..........................36, 37
Belief........9, 14, 28, 31, 38, 39
Beneficial...........................18
Benefit. .10, 14, 15, 17, 20, 21,
    24
Betray.................................39
Bible Study Guides................4
Biblically correct....................8
Biting and devouring............39
Born of God, being..............38
Brotherhood35, 36, 37, 38, 39,
    40
Brotherly affection...............35
Building, edifying......12, 18, 37
Burden...........................24, 36
Burdens..............................36
Care.......................19, 21, 36
Carson, Don..........................9
Chemosh.............................30
Christian hedonism..............20
Church discipline 11, 12, 13, 30
Church unity........................32
Circumspection....................39
Club....................................18
Commands...23, 24, 28, 35, 38

Commitment18, 19, 29, 30, 31,
    32, 39
Communicants...................7, 8
Complaints..........................37
Conceit..........................37, 39
Confession...............7, 31, 37
Confidence..............9, 21, 34
Consumer......................15, 20
Contextualised....................18
Controlling............................8
Converted......................14, 17
Copyright...............................2
Covenant..........................2, 4
Covenant Books UK..........1, 2
Credible profession of faith.15,
    18
Creeds..................................9
Criticism..............................32
Cross, the.........................2, 31
Culturally alien...............15, 18
Culturally appropriate.....17, 27
Culture.................4, 10, 17, 30
Damascus............................14
David, King........................2, 4
Deacon...........................11, 21
Decisions............................27
Defeater belief......................9
Deprivation.........................36
Disagree.............................39
Disciple...10, 11, 14, 15, 28, 35
Discipleship-Lite..................28
Division...............................36
Doing good..........................40
Don'ts.................................23
Don'ts...........................25, 39
Dos'.............................23, 35
Each other, verses..11, 24, 29,
    32, 35, 36, 37, 39
Edification...........................36
Ekklēsia, see Ἐκκλησία.......29
Elder.........................9, 11, 32

Encouragement. .4, 19, 24, 35,
    36, 37
Endurance...........................36
Envy....................................40
ESV........................2, 24, 34
Evangelical............................7
Evangelist............................15
Excommunication...............12
Faith 15, 18, 20, 21, 30, 31, 35,
    37
Falsehood............................36
Family.......................4, 19, 22
Fear....................................27
Fedora...................................2
Fellowship........7, 11, 15, 19, 38
Fighting...............................39
Finances..............................27
Flesh...................................36
Forgiveness....................22, 37
Freedom...........................8, 36
Friendship...........................19
Gentile...........................11, 12
Gentleness...........................36
Geographical location...........11
Glory.....................32, 36, 39
Godliness..............................9
Golf club.............................17
Good standing.....................21
Goodness.............................36
Gospel, the good news.11, 20,
    22
Gossip................................32
Grace..................................38
Greeting..........................9, 36
Grumbling.................38, 39, 40
Harmony.............................35
Hate.............................39, 40
Hating.................................40
Haughtiness........................35
Health, wealth and prosperity
   20

Healthy relationships............32
Heart...7, 10, 29, 30, 35, 37, 38
Heavy shepherding...............27
Hindrance............................36
Holy Spirit, the..........14, 20, 31
Holy Trinity, the......................9
Honour................................35
Hospitality...........................38
Humble................................35
Humility...30, 32, 36, 37, 38, 40
Humour..................................4
Importance.............................8
Individualism...........................8
Interview................................9
Jerusalem................13, 14, 15
Jesus 8, 10, 11, 12, 13, 14, 20,
    21, 28, 29, 31, 35, 36, 38,
    39
Jew...............................11, 14
Job......................................20
Join.12, 14, 15, 17, 18, 19, 20,
    21, 22, 24, 27, 28, 29, 30
Join fn..................................13
Join, in membership 12, 13, 14,
    15, 17, 18, 19, 20, 21, 22,
    27, 29, 30
Joy............7, 14, 17, 20, 24, 34
Joy..1
Judgement............................39
Judging..................36, 39, 40
Keller, Tim..............................9
Kindness.........................22, 37
Kingdom of God 10, 19, 30, 32,
    34
Knowledge............................36
Kollaophobia.......21, 22, 27, 30
Law......................2, 4, 36, 40
Leaders....................24, 30, 32
Light, the.................20, 21, 38
List, of members.7, 17, 18, 19,
    21
Lord's supper...................7, 39
Love..7, 21, 22, 23, 29, 32, 35,
    36, 37, 38, 39
Lowly....................................35
Lying.................9, 15, 18, 37
Malice.................................40
Marriage........................22, 36
Maturity................4, 21, 22

Means of grace.........19, 20, 34
Meeting................9, 13, 21, 37
Members, existing......9, 17, 32
Middle class..........................17
Naomi......................28, 29, 30
Neighbour........................7, 37
New commandment.......35, 38
New member..9, 20, 30, 31, 32
NIV..........2, 24, 34, 36, 37, 39
Non-Christian...........12, 13, 23
Non-communicants............7, 8
Non-members..................8, 20
Nonconformist.........................7
Obedience............................37
Old fashioned........................18
One another, verses 24, 29, 35,
    36, 37, 38, 39, 40
Opportunities........................19
Owing, debt....................36, 39
Passions and pleasures.......40
Patience..............................36
Paul, apostle...............8, 11, 21
Peace..............1, 34, 36, 39
Perfect church.......................30
Person-hood............................8
Piper, John...........................20
Politically correct....................8
Post-modern...........................8
Post-modernism......................8
Practical.........................19, 32
Pray, praying, prayer....19, 32,
    36, 37
Preaching............................14
Prescriptive.............................8
Pride....................................27
Promises..............9, 24, 30, 31
Proud, pride..........................38
Provoking.............................39
Quiet times..........................22
Reality....................................8
Reliability..............................21
Remembering.................35, 40
Responsibility.................19, 21
Revelation..............................8
Revenge...............................40
Reverence............................37
Revival............................7, 8
Righteousness.......1, 4, 10, 34
Roll, of members............4, 7, 8

Rules...............................17, 23
Ruth..........8, 28, 29, 30, 37, 38
Sacrament..................7, 11, 19
Salvation..............................31
Satan....................................36
Saul................13, 14, 15, 17
Self-reliance..........................31
Selfishness.....................20, 37
Sense of belonging...............19
Sermons................................9
Service...............7, 8, 9, 21, 35
Sexual immorality.................39
Sharing........................2, 7, 20
Sin....8, 10, 12, 13, 22, 30, 31,
    37, 38, 40
Sin of omission....................10
Small Groups..........................4
Social media..........................18
Speaking evil........................40
Stephen................................29
Stir up to good works............37
Stumbling block....................36
Stunting, of growth...............19
Submission...24, 27, 30, 32, 37
Substitutionary atonement....31
Support...............12, 17, 19, 32
Tax collector..........................12
Teaching...............9, 10, 12, 28
Tender-hearted......................37
Thanksgiving.........................37
Threatening............................8
Time....................................27
Timothy................................21
Trusting in Christ..................31
Truth..........................8, 37, 38
Universal church 10, 11, 12, 13,
    14, 15
Warnings........................24, 39
Washing feet.........................35
Welcome..................9, 32, 36
Western..........................17, 18
Wisdom............2, 8, 35, 39
Women's Institute.................17
World-view..............................8
'Dos'....................................24
'Righteousness,.....................1
"Don'ts"................................24
Ἐκκλησία..................9, 12, 29

Scripture Index

Ruth 1:16.................pp28,29
Ruth 1:17.........................p29
Psalms 120.......................p4
Proverbs 12:20................p34
Matthew 6:33....................p10
Matthew 16:18.................p12
Matthew 18:16..........pp12,15
Matthew 24:10.................p39
Matthew 28:19.........pp15,28
Matthew 28:20 ....p28
Mark 9:34.........................p39
Mark 9:50.........................p39
Luke 16:10.......................p20
Luke 16:13.......................p21
Luke 16:16.......................p30
Luke 24:14.......................p35
Luke 24:32.......................p35
John 3:16.........................p22
John 5:43.........................p39
John 6:43.........................p39
John 13:14.................pp24,35
John 13:15.......................p23
John 13:34-35..........pp24,35
Acts.................pp12,13,15
Acts 2:41,47; 5:14............p13
Acts 5..............................p13
Acts 5:11..........................p13
Acts 5:12..........................p13
Acts 5:12b........................p13
Acts 7..............................p29
Acts 7:26..........................p39
Acts 9.............pp13,14,15,17
Acts 9:20-22.....................p14
Acts 9:26a................pp14,17
Acts 9:26b........................p14
Acts 9:27..........................p15

Acts 13:9..........................p17
Acts 15:39........................p39
Acts 20:35.............pp4,20,21
Acts 28:4..........................p39
Romans 1:12.............pp24,35
Romans 1:27....................p39
Romans 12:5....................p35
Romans 12:10..................p35
Romans 12:16..................p35
Romans 13:8....................p36
Romans 14:13..................p36
Romans 14:17...........pp4,34
Romans 14:19..................p36
Romans 15:5....................p36
Romans 15:7.............pp30,36
Romans 15:14..................p36
Romans 16:5.............pp9,12
Romans 16:16..................p36
1 Corinthians 5:12-13.......p13
1 Corinthians 7:5..............p36
1 Corinthians 11:33..........p39
1 Corinthians 12:25..........p36
1 Corinthians 16:19..........p12
Galatians 5:13..................p36
Galatians 5:15..................p39
Galatians 5:22..................p34
Galatians 6:2....................p36
Ephesians.........................p4
Ephesians 3:6..................p11
Ephesians 4:2..................p36
Ephesians 4:13................p21
Ephesians 4:25................p36
Ephesians 4:32................p37
Ephesians 5:21-6:9..........p37
Ephesians 5:21................p37
Ephesians 5:25................p18

Philippians 2:3.................p37
Philippians 3:17...............p23
Colossians 3:9.................p37
Colossians 3:13...............p37
1 Thessalonians 3:12.......p37
1 Thessalonians 4:9.........p37
1 Thessalonians 4:18; 5:11
.............................p37
1 Thessalonians 5:15.......p40
2 Thessalonians 1:3.........p37
1 Timothy 3:8-13.......pp21,34
Titus 3:3...........................p40
Philemon 2.......................p12
Hebrews...........................p24
Hebrews 2:13; 6:9; 13:18. p24
Hebrews 5:13...................p34
Hebrews 10:22; 11:1.......p34
Hebrews 10:24-25............p37
Hebrews 12:22.................p11
Hebrews 13:17a...............p24
Hebrews 13:17b...............p24
James 4:11.......................p40
James 5:9.........................p40
James 5:16.......................p37
1 Peter 1:22.....................p37
1 Peter 4:9.......................p38
1 Peter 5:1-5....................p27
1 Peter 5:5.......................p38
1 John 1:7........................p38
1 John 3:11.......................p38
1 John 3:23.......................p38
1 John 4:7........................p38
1 John 4:11.......................p38
1 John 4:12.............pp29,38
2 John 5...........................p38
Jude 23............................p22

Also available on Amazon and other sellers:

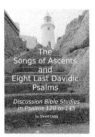

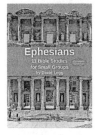

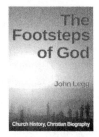

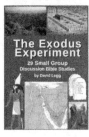

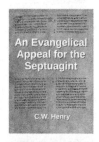

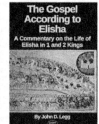

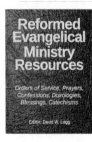

Printed in Great Britain
by Amazon

38879318R00030